Free Dive

by Stephen Rickard

Published by Ransom Publishing Ltd.
51 Southgate Street, Winchester, Hampshire SO23 9EH
www.ransom.co.uk

ISBN   978 184167 782 8

First published in 2010

Copyright © 2010 Ransom Publishing Ltd.

All photographs are copyright © 2009: front cover, page 25 - Dan Zalgaler; inside front cover, pages 4/5, 14/15, 18/19, 20/21 - Dan Burton; title page, pages 26, 27, 28, 29, 30/31, 32/33 - Igor Liberti; pages 6/7 - Graeme Fordham; pages 8/9 - Miha Urbanija; pages 22, 23, 24 - Annelie Pompe; back cover, pages 34/35 - Deborah Metcalfe, Blue Eye FX; pages 12, 13, 16/17, 36 - theblueproject.org; inside back cover - Rami Ben Ami.

A CIP catalogue record of this book is available from the British Library.

The right of Stephen Rickard to be identified as the author of this Work has been asserted by him in accordance with sections 77 and 78 of the Copyright, Design and Patents Act 1988.

FREE DIVE

STEPHEN RICHARD

Ransom

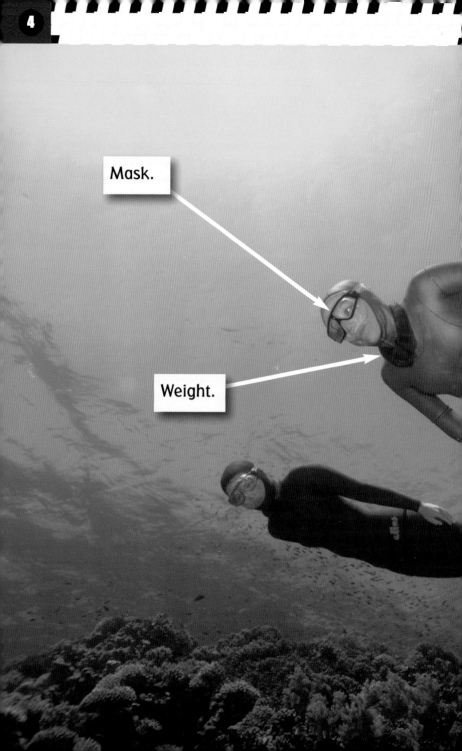

Mask.

Weight.

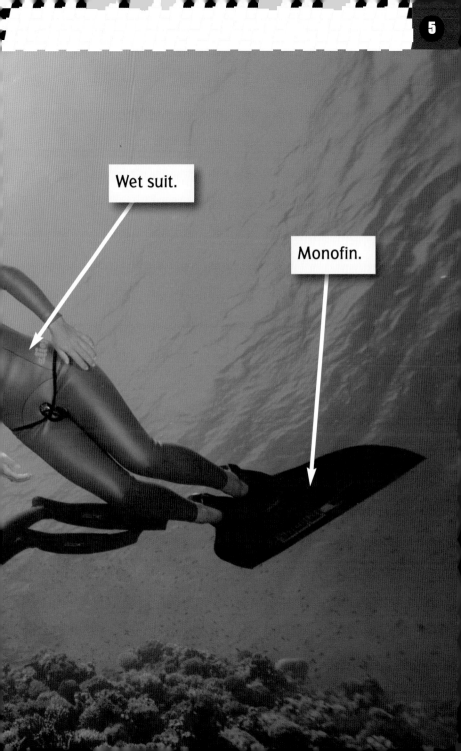

Wet suit.

Monofin.

Hi. I'm Sara Campbell.

I am a free diver.

In free diving you must swim as deep as you can - and them come back to the surface.

You don't take any air with you, so you must hold your breath the whole time.

This is where I live. It's a place called Dahab, in Egypt.

It's near the Red Sea.

Dahab is great for free diving.

There is a very good place to dive here.

The place is called Blue Hole.

The water there is deep but very still.

It's perfect for free diving.

I am very good at free diving. I hold four world records.

I am also a World Champion free diver.

But you can see that I'm very small.

I'm less than 5 feet tall.

People call me 'Mighty Mouse'.

When I dive, I wear a big fin.

It's called a monofin.

The monofin helps me swim with less effort. So I will use less oxygen.

That means I can stay under the water for longer. So I can dive even deeper.

I train a lot in the water.

With my monofin, I swim like a dolphin.

It is great being in the water. I love it. It makes me so happy.

I can hold my breath for 3 minutes 36 seconds.

That's when I'm swimming at the same time.

But free diving is dangerous.

You must take care.

You must **never**, **ever**, free dive on your own.

Somebody must **always** be with you.

blue

CLIMATE AND OCEANS PROJECT

When you dive deep, the water pressure makes your lungs very small.

Your eardrums can burst, too.

But this is not the worst that can happen.

Free diving is most dangerous when you come back up to the surface.

Near the surface your lungs are expanding and you are running out of breath.

This is when you can pass out.

It's called a blackout.

If you have a blackout, your dive doesn't count.

So you don't want this to happen.

Having a blackout is just like a computer shutting down when it runs out of power.

A blackout is to protect your brain.

But still, it is not a good thing to happen.

I have blacked out three times.

This is why you must **never**, **ever**, free dive or practise holding your breath on your own.

Somebody must always be with you.

To be a good free diver, you must train your body.

But you must train your mind, too.

This is most important.

You must think that you can dive deep.

You must **KNOW** that you can dive deep.

I practise holding my breath in the water.

When you try to break a free dive record, you must follow a rope down.

Other divers are there too. They make sure you are OK.

Now you can see me doing my world record dive.

I dived to 96.6 metres. That's as long as a football pitch.

I had to follow the rope all the way down.

The other divers cannot go as deep as I need to. It's not safe for them.

So I am on my own.

It takes me just over 1 minute 30 seconds to get the the bottom.

At the bottom, I pick up a tag. I must bring it to the surface.

It proves how deep I dived.

Then I have to get back up.

I have been holding my breath for more than two minutes now.

I carry a weight around my neck.

This helps me dive down quickly.

But getting back up is harder.

This is the dangerous part. I might pass out.

The divers have been waiting for me.

They watch me carefully.

Will I be OK?

I get to the surface.

I have the tag.

And I didn't pass out.

And here is the proof.
96.6 metres.

No other woman has dived so deep on one breath.

It feels great. Really great.

But already a little bit of me is thinking about the next step: a dive to beat 100 metres ...

JARGON BUSTER

black out
dolphin
goggles
monofin

pressure
weight
yoga